CHILDHOOD FEARS AND ANXIETIES

MEDICAL FEARS

CHILDHOOD FEARS
AND ANXIETIES

Anxiety and Fear in Daily Life

Catastrophes

Crime and Terrorism

Family Fears

Medical Fears

Nighttime Fears

Phobias

School Fears

Separation Anxiety

Social Fears

Symptoms and Treatments of
Anxiety Disorders

CHILDHOOD FEARS
AND ANXIETIES

MEDICAL FEARS

H.W. POOLE

SERIES CONSULTANT
ANNE S. WALTERS, Ph.D.

Emma Pendleton Bradley Hospital

Warren Alpert Medical School of
Brown University

MASON CREST

Mason Crest
450 Parkway Drive, Suite D
Broomall, PA 19008
www.masoncrest.com

MTM Publishing, Inc.
435 West 23rd Street, #8C
New York, NY 10011
www.mtmpublishing.com

President: Valerie Tomaselli
Vice President, Book Development: Hilary Poole
Designer: Annemarie Redmond
Copyeditor: Peter Jaskowiak
Editorial Assistant: Leigh Eron

Series ISBN: 978-1-4222-3721-2
Hardback ISBN: 978-1-4222-3726-7
E-Book ISBN: 978-1-4222-8059-1

Library of Congress Cataloging-in-Publication Data
Names: Poole, Hilary W., author. | Walters, Anne S., consultant.
Title: Medical fears / by H.W. Poole ; Series consultant, Anne S. Walters, Ph.D., Emma Pendleton Bradley Hospital, Alpert Medical School/Brown University.
Description: Broomall, PA: Mason Crest, [2018] | Series: Childhood fears and anxieties | Audience: Ages 12+. | Audience: Grades 7-8. | Includes bibliographical references and index.
Identifiers: LCCN 2016053115 (print) | LCCN 2017002817 (ebook) | ISBN 9781422237267 (hardback alk. paper) | ISBN 9781422280591 (ebook)
Subjects: LCSH: Fear in children—Juvenile literature. | Fear of doctors—Juvenile literature. | Fear of medical care—Juvenile literature. | Anxiety in children—Juvenile literature. | Anxiety disorders—Juvenile literature. | Child psychology—Juvenile literature.
Classification: LCC BF723.F4 P66 2018 (print) | LCC BF723.F4 (ebook) | DDC 618.92/8522—dc23
LC record available at https://lccn.loc.gov/2016053115

Printed and bound in the United States of America.

First printing
9 8 7 6 5 4 3 2 1

TABLE OF CONTENTS

Series Introduction 6

Chapter One: Fear and Health 9

Chapter Two: Doctors, Dentists, and Therapists 19

Chapter Three: Places and Procedures 27

Chapter Four: Conquering Medical Fears 35

Further Reading 44

Series Glossary 45

Index 47

About the Advisor 48

About the Author 48

Photo Credits 48

Key Icons to Look for:

 Words to Understand: These words with their easy-to-understand definitions will increase the reader's understanding of the text, while building vocabulary skills.

 Sidebars: This boxed material within the main text allows readers to build knowledge, gain insights, explore possibilities, and broaden their perspectives by weaving together additional information to provide realistic and holistic perspectives.

 Educational Videos: Readers can view videos by scanning our QR codes, which will provide them with additional educational content to supplement the text. Examples include news coverage, moments in history, speeches, iconic sports moments, and much more.

 Text-Dependent Questions: These questions send the reader back to the text for more careful attention to the evidence presented there.

 Research Projects: Readers are pointed toward areas of further inquiry connected to each chapter. Suggestions are provided for projects that encourage deeper research and analysis.

Series Glossary of Key Terms: This back-of-the-book glossary contains terminology used throughout the series. Words found here increase the reader's ability to read and comprehend higher-level books and articles in this field.

SERIES INTRODUCTION

Who among us does not have memories of an intense childhood fear? Fears and anxieties are a part of *every* childhood. Indeed, these fears are fodder for urban legends and campfire tales alike. And while the details of these legends and tales change over time, they generally have at their base predictable childhood terrors such as darkness, separation from caretakers, or bodily injury.

We know that fear has an evolutionary component. Infants are helpless, and, compared to other mammals, humans have a very long developmental period. Fear ensures that curious children will stay close to caretakers, making them less likely to be exposed to danger. This means that childhood fears are adaptive, making us more likely to survive, and even thrive, as a species.

Unfortunately, there comes a point when fear and anxiety cease to be useful. This is especially problematic today, for there has been a startling increase in anxiety among children and adolescents. In fact, 25 percent of 13- to 18-year-olds now have mild to moderate anxiety, and the *median* age of onset for anxiety disorders is just 11 years old.

Why might this be? Some say that the contemporary United States is a nation preoccupied with risk, and it is certainly possible that our children are absorbing this preoccupation as well. Certainly, our exposure to potential threats has never been greater. We see graphic images via the media and have more immediate news of all forms of disaster. This can lead our children to feel more vulnerable, and it may increase the likelihood that they respond with fear. If children based their fear on the news that they see on Facebook or on TV, they would dramatically overestimate the likelihood of terrible things happening.

As parents or teachers, what do we do about fear? As in other areas of life, we provide our children with guidance and education on a daily basis. We teach them about the signs and feelings of fear. We discuss and normalize typical fear reactions, and support them in tackling difficult situations despite fear. We explain—and demonstrate by example—how to identify "negative thinking traps" and generate positive coping thoughts instead.

But to do so effectively, we might need to challenge some of our own assumptions about fear. Adults often assume that they must protect their children from fear and help them to avoid scary situations, when sometimes the best course is for the child to face the fear and conquer it. This is counterintuitive for many adults: after all, isn't it our job to reassure our children and help them feel better? Yes, of course! Except when it isn't. Sometimes they need us to help them confront their fears and move forward anyway.

That's where these volumes come in. When it comes to fear, balanced information is critical. Learning about fear as it relates to many different areas can help us to help our children remember that although you don't choose whether to be afraid, you do choose how to handle it. These volumes explore the world of childhood fears, seeking to answer important questions: How much is too much? And how can fear be positive, functioning to mobilize us in the face of danger?

Fear gives us the opportunity to step up and respond with courage and resilience. It pushes us to expand our sphere of functioning to areas that might feel unfamiliar or risky. When we are a little nervous or afraid, we tend to prepare a little more, look for more information, ask more questions—and all of this can function to help us expand the boundaries of our lives in a positive direction. So, while fear might *feel* unpleasant, there is no doubt that it can have a positive outcome.

Let's teach our children that.

—Anne Walters, Ph.D.
Chief Psychologist, Emma Pendleton Bradley Hospital
Clinical Associate Professor,
Alpert Medical School of Brown University

CHAPTER ONE

FEAR AND HEALTH

Everyone feels afraid sometimes. This has been true since the time of the earliest humans, and it will still be true long after we are gone. Fear is a survival skill. Our ancient ancestors feared predators, and they feared darkness because predators could hide there. Today, fear keeps us (well, most of us!) from taking unnecessary risks. Whether it's climbing too high, driving too fast, or insulting people more powerful than ourselves, we tend to avoid actions that could result in us getting hurt. The ability to feel fear is a tool for self-preservation. In that sense, fear is a healthy emotion.

That is how things are supposed to work. But sometimes our fears are unhealthy. Take **agoraphobia**, for example. People who have this condition are afraid to leave their homes. If you don't leave home, you can't go to school, you can't do basic things like shop for groceries or clothes, and you miss out on social activities. Agoraphobia

WORDS TO UNDERSTAND

agoraphobia: an intense fear of being in public spaces.

communicable: an illness that can be spread by contact between people.

intimidating: causing someone to feel nervous or inadequate.

preventive: keeping something from happening.

is not healthy at all: it seriously affects overall well-being and mental health. You are not likely to have a satisfying life if fear keeps you trapped inside your house. When we say agoraphobia is "not healthy," we don't mean that it's unhealthy the way the flu is unhealthy. We mean that it's not a happy or satisfying way to live.

However, when it comes to medical fears, we actually *do* mean "unhealthy" the way the flu is unhealthy. If your fear keeps you from seeing the doctor when you need to, then medical fears can literally make you sick.

WHAT ARE MEDICAL FEARS

Medical fears come in many shapes and sizes. Most are caused by a few things: fear of the unknown, fear of not being in control, and fear of pain or suffering. We can group specific medical fears into a few different categories.

Fear of Illness. Nobody wants to get sick, and it's understandable that someone might want to avoid people who are sick. But sometimes the fear of getting sick is so intense that people avoid friends and family who are ill. This might make sense if the sick person has the flu, but a fear of illness makes some individuals avoid people with cancer or other conditions that are not communicable.

Other people avoid going to the doctor simply because they are too scared of hearing bad news. In

EDUCATIONAL VIDEO

Scan this code for a video about the causes of medical fears.

other words, they would prefer to pretend that they aren't sick rather than risk hearing the truth that they are. On the other hand, some people react in the opposite way—they are so afraid of being sick that they start thinking that every little cough or muscle ache is the end of the world.

Fear of Doctors. With their white coats and technical language, doctors themselves make some people very anxious. Other people are okay with doctors but are afraid of dentists or mental health providers. All these folks can be intimidating because they know about all kinds of things that we don't. We worry that they will judge us for unhealthy things that we do. Also, doctors make

Some people are so afraid of getting sick that they avoid other people who are.

decisions about tests, medications, and procedures that we don't always understand—and some of those procedures hurt!

Fear of Doctors' Offices and Hospitals. Sometimes it's not so much the people that make us afraid, but the places where they work. Whether it's the doctor's office, the dentist's chair, or the hospital, these places are often filled with confusing, scary-looking equipment. They may smell strange. Other people get nervous just going near a hospital—after all, there are lots of people in hospitals who are sick, in pain, or even dying.

Fear of Physical Exams. Going to the doctor frequently involves getting undressed. You've probably experienced this: you go into an exam

Dental exams involve a stranger putting her or his hands in your mouth.

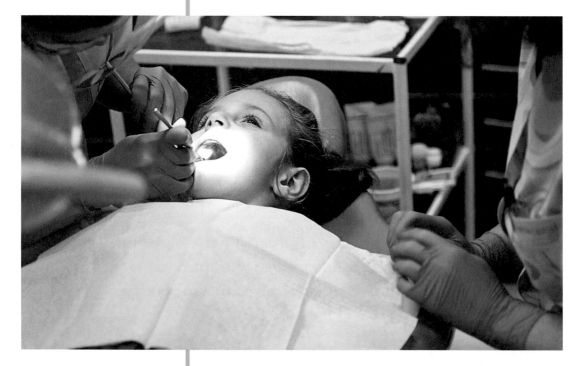

SYMPTOMS OF MEDICAL FEARS

There is nothing wrong with feeling a little bit nervous about doctors and dentists. But some people are a lot more than a little nervous. Here are some signs that medical fears might be bigger than average and that you might need help to overcome them:

- You make up excuses why you can't go to the appointment.
- You have trouble sleeping the night (or even nights) before the appointment.
- You want to cry if you even think about the appointment.
- You feel intensely nervous or stressed out the day of the appointment.
- You feel upset or sick at the sight of health-care providers or equipment.
- You panic before or during procedures.

room and you have to take your clothes off and put on one of those gowns that never fit quite right. Lots of people don't like feeling exposed in this way. Then, the doctor usually has to touch you—sometimes in intimate places—and that can be very upsetting for some people.

Meanwhile, at the dentist's office, you don't have to get undressed, but you have someone sitting extremely close to you and putting his or her hands in your mouth. This makes some people uncomfortable.

Fear of Procedures and Tests. Another common fear many people have is of whatever might happen to them when they are in the office or hospital. Some tests are embarrassing or uncomfortable. Others seem mysterious or just downright weird. For example, what's the deal with that X-ray machine, anyway? What does it do? These kinds of questions can make people very anxious.

Fear of Needles. This is a fear many kids know well because of vaccinations. Nobody actually enjoys getting a shot, of course, but some people have such an intense fear of needles that it is extremely upsetting to them. Sometimes the fear is so bad that people avoid getting their vaccinations completely.

WHAT'S THE BIG DEAL?

If you have one of the fears mentioned above, you might be wondering, "So what? If doctors or dentists bother you, don't go."

The truth is, a lot of adults do exactly that. There is a term for it: *doctor avoidance.* This means choosing to not go to the doctor when you know you should. In a 2014 study, researchers found that about one-third of adults were guilty of doctor avoidance.

Doctor avoidance is a bad idea for a number of reasons. First, the most important thing doctors and dentists can provide is called preventive care. Preventive care is pretty much what it sounds like— getting medical help to stop you from getting sick in the first place. Regular check-ups can catch tiny

WHAT IS PREVENTIVE CARE?

We keep talking about the importance of preventive care, but what is it, *really*? You know what the phrase means in a general sense: preventive care is health care that helps keep you from getting sick. But what does that involve?

- **Health promotion.** The most important things that anyone can do to stay healthy are pretty simple: don't smoke, do exercise, get enough sleep, and eat healthy. We know this, but we don't always follow through. The things doctors and nurses do to encourage these healthy choices are vital parts of preventive care.
- **Screenings.** In health care, the word *screening* refers to any kind of basic test to check for a possible illness. Kids are screened for vision and hearing problems, as well as for potential problems with their blood cells and the growth of their spines. Adults get screenings for cancer and other problems.
- **Vaccinations.** Although they do hurt a tiny bit, vaccinations save lives.
- **Early diagnosis.** Sometimes a person will have what seems like a minor symptom that is actually a sign of something more serious. Doctors ask a lot of questions during check-ups because they are looking for tiny signals of future problems.

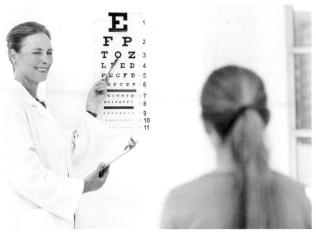

Vision screening is one important type of preventive care.

RESEARCH PROJECT

Find out about preventive care for people at different ages: babies, kids, teens, adults, and the elderly. What types of procedures and tests are recommended for each group? Why are they recommended? Make a booklet with a page for each age group that lists the procedures. (You can find lists of preventive care at the websites HealthCare.gov and MedlinePlus.gov, and many more.)

problems before they become big ones. Regular teeth cleanings can stop painful dental problems before they start. If you think about it, isn't that a thousand times better than waiting until you are already miserable?

When you do get sick (it happens to everybody!), the sooner you get help, the sooner you will feel better. Yes, it's true that some illnesses go away on their own. But in most cases, a visit to a doctor can help speed along your recovery. And where teeth are concerned, problems like cavities are definitely *not* going away on their own.

SO WHAT DO I DO?

When people talk about medical fears, they sometimes try to separate out being afraid of people who do medicine (doctors, dentists, therapists) from being afraid of the places where they do it (offices, hospitals) or the actual things they do (tests, needles, drills). But fear isn't always so clear-cut. You might feel anxious but not really know whether it's the doctor, the office, or the needle that is making you nervous. It might be all those things!

In the rest of this book, we are going to take some of these different fears and look at them separately. Thinking through the different fears may help you better understand what exactly is bothering you. The better you understand your feelings, the better able you'll be to do something about them.

Being nervous about medical issues is totally normal. But you want to make sure that unhealthy levels of anxiety don't rob you of the mental and physical health you deserve.

It's not always easy to figure out the exact source of a medical fear.

 TEXT-DEPENDENT QUESTIONS

1. What are some types of medical fears?

2. What are some reasons people have medical fears?

3. What is preventive care?

CHAPTER TWO

DOCTORS, DENTISTS, AND THERAPISTS

For some people, simply being around medical professionals makes them nervous. There's even a name for this: white-coat **syndrome**. This name refers to the type of coats doctors are known for wearing. One study suggested that as many as one in five adults has some degree of white-coat syndrome. So if you feel anxious or even scared of your doctor, dentist, or therapist, you are not alone.

WHY DOES THIS HAPPEN?

If you asked 100 people with white-coat syndrome why they feel the way they do, you would probably get 100 slightly different answers. But there are some common threads we can name. One is simply the fact that doctors are authority figures. They attended school for many years to learn a massive amount of information. It can feel weird to talk to someone who

WORDS TO UNDERSTAND

confidential: private; something that can't be shared.

psychological: having to do with the mind and thoughts.

syndrome: a condition.

HONESTY IS THE BEST POLICY

Most of us have experienced a moment when our doctors asked us questions we didn't want to answer. Your pediatrician might ask about junk food or screen time. Your dentist might ask how often you brush your teeth. If you are seeing a therapist, he or she will ask lots of questions about how you feel and what you think. It's important to answer all these questions truthfully. Doctors are there to help you. They need to know what's really going on—even if the truth is embarrassing.

Try to view your appointment as an *opportunity*. If you lie, you are turning down the opportunity to make your life better. That doesn't make much sense, does it? Your doctor is not your parent, priest, or teacher. Doctors do not judge whether their patients are good people or not. They are not going to be mad, or disappointed, or send you to junk-food jail.

Doctors have to keep what you tell them **confidential**. Yes, even kids have the right to private conversations with their doctors. (The only time this isn't the case is if something is going on in your life that affects your safety.)

Finally, remember that your doctor has seen many other patients before you came along. Those patients had the same kinds of problems you do, and they made the same kinds of mistakes. Whatever "bad" thing you think you've done, your doctor has already seen it, and in most cases, he or she has seen a lot worse! So don't worry about shocking your doctor. Just tell the truth and let him or her help you do better in the future.

knows so much more than you do—especially when the subject you're discussing is your own body!

People also get anxious because they are afraid of being judged. For example, you probably know that your doctor doesn't want you to spend too many hours in front of your computer or TV ("screen time"). Sitting for really long periods is bad for your body, staring at screens can be bad for your eyes, and spending time interacting with videos rather than humans can be bad for your overall development. You might worry that your doctor will be disappointed or even angry if you admit to too much screen time. This can cause anxiety when it is time for your check-up. (Tell the truth anyway! See the box on page 20 for more on being honest with your doctor.)

Some people have had bad experiences that stick with them. Maybe they were hurt in some way, or they felt like someone didn't care about them or didn't do a good job. Or maybe they have just heard

Doctors wear gloves to protect both their patients and themselves, but some kids find them scary.

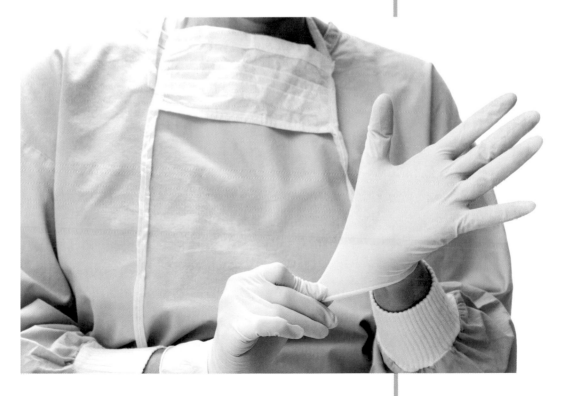

bad stories from friends or family members. Even the media can contribute to white-coat syndrome. You don't have to look very hard to find news stories about a surgery that went wrong or some other medical catastrophe.

Last but not least, the ways health care is delivered can make all these anxious feelings worse. Doctors tend to be very busy, and they may only spend a little bit of time with each patient. Because health insurance remains quite expensive in the United States, people change insurance plans frequently, which can mean switching doctors. The result is a lot of overwhelmed doctors who lack long-term relationships with their patients.

DENTISTS

White-coat syndrome is especially strong when it comes to dentists. Between 9 and 15 percent of Americans say they avoid the dentist because of anxiety. Some people even live with bad dental problems, such as bleeding gums and sore or missing teeth, simply because they are afraid of going to the dentist.

Maybe it's because even regular cleanings can be physically uncomfortable. You have to lean back in an awkward way. You have to hold your mouth open for an unnaturally long period. You feel helpless because you have to just lie there with no control over what happens to you. Meanwhile, someone you

EDUCATIONAL VIDEO

Scan this code for a video about kids overcoming their fear of doctors.

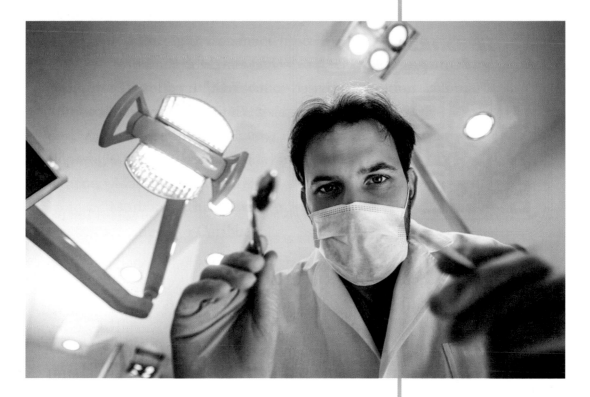

barely know puts his or her hands in your mouth! And if you have a cavity or other problems, there may be pain involved.

Unfortunately, this is what's sometimes called a vicious circle. Avoiding the dentist means that when you do go, you will probably need more work done. The result is that the visit is longer and more uncomfortable than it would have been if you had gone sooner. When you do go, you're tense. Being tense can actually make the dental experience more painful than it would have been if you were relaxed. But then that pain just provides evidence that the dentist's office is a scary place and you were right to avoid it. Then the whole cycle starts again.

Let's face it: a trip to the dentist is just not high on anybody's list of "fun" activities.

RESEARCH PROJECT

Create a survey about medical fears. Ask questions like: "did you ever avoid a sick person?"; "do you avoid the doctor or dentist?"; "do you worry before appointments?"; "what do you worry about?" Add more questions if you can think of any. Survey people of different ages, and tally the answers based on the age of the people you spoke to. Did younger people have the same fears as older ones, or were they different?

THERAPISTS

If you fall off your skateboard and break your leg, it will pretty obvious that you need a doctor. But sometimes people need help with problems that aren't physical, but **psychological**—meaning problems that involve our thoughts and feelings. There are a lot of different types of things that can happen, but for kids, the most common problems are feeling anxious and scared all (or most of) the time, feeling depressed or sad for long periods, or having more angry feelings than you can handle. Other times, psychological problems can come from outside the person rather than inside—like if your parents get divorced or someone close to you dies. Moving to a new house, having a parent in jail or in the military, or being severely bullied are all outside factors that can cause psychological problems for kids. Sometimes, the overall stress of dealing with school and friends can feel like more than you can handle.

When these problems arise, you might need to talk to a therapist. There are a few different types, but they all do more-or-less the same thing: they talk to you about your problems, thoughts, and feelings. They help you understand yourself better, and they try to help you figure out strategies to deal with hard times. Some therapists also prescribe medication, while others don't do that.

Going to the therapist for the first time can be scary, mostly because it's a new experience. You

have been going to the doctor and the dentist your whole life, but that's usually not true with a therapist. See chapter four for tips about how to cope with this anxiety.

Talking to a therapist can make you feel exposed emotionally, rather than physically.

 TEXT-DEPENDENT QUESTIONS

1. What's a nickname for the fear of doctors?

2. How many Americans avoid going to the dentist because of fear?

3. Why do people see therapists?

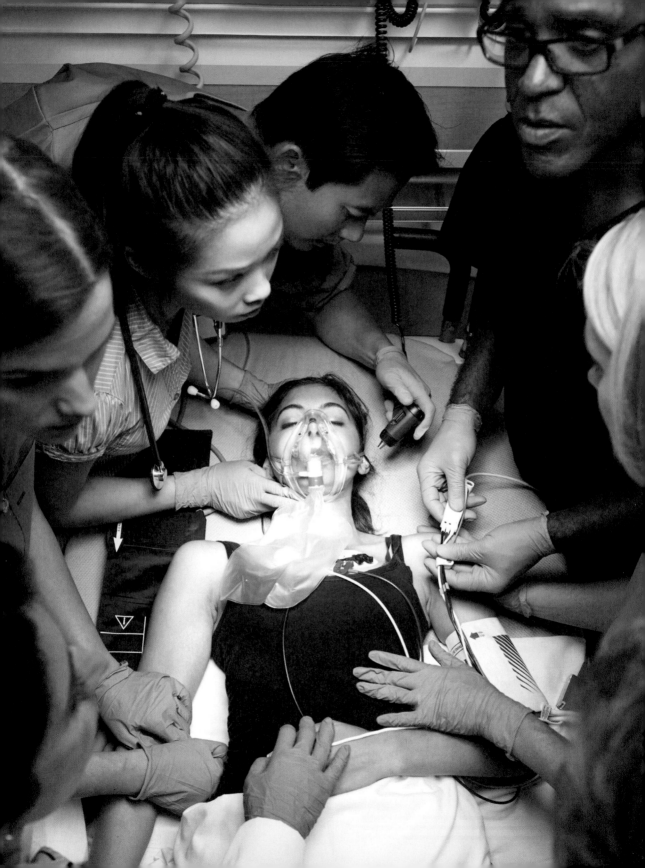

CHAPTER THREE

PLACES AND PROCEDURES

Whether they are doctors, dentists, or therapists, medical professionals can be intimidating. But in reality, most of them—*especially* the ones who choose to work with kids—are perfectly nice people. Unfortunately, even the world's nicest doctor may have to stick you with a needle or do some other procedure that you don't like very much. So even if you don't fear the specific doctor, there are still lots of other things that might make you anxious.

HOSPITALS AND DOCTORS' OFFICES

There is a lot about a hospital that makes people uncomfortable. Hospitals tend to be large, busy places. There are all kinds of people rushing around. They always smell a little weird—mostly due to the strong cleaning products used to keep everything **sanitary**. And finally, hospitals are, by definition, full of sick people. Sometimes people go to the hospital

WORDS TO UNDERSTAND

colonoscopy: a procedure that allows a doctor to look inside the digestive system.

diagnosis: determining what exactly is causing a particular illness or condition.

sanitary: clean; free from anything that might cause illness.

and never come back. If you feel that hospitals are bad places where bad stuff happens, you aren't alone. A lot of people dislike or even fear hospitals.

It is important to remember that while bad things do happen sometimes, a lot of great things happen in hospitals, too. In fact, the number of people who go to the hospital and get better is a *lot* bigger than

Hospitals can be big, intimidating places.

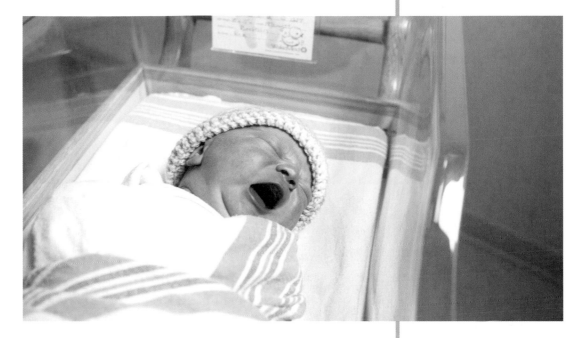

the number of people who don't. People survive cancer and have tumors removed, they recover from pneumonia, and on and on. Babies are born in hospitals! The human brain is wired to focus on bad things, but the reality is that more good things happen in hospitals than bad.

PROCEDURES

You are probably more familiar with your doctor's and dentist's offices than with the hospital. Of course, that means you are more familiar with the unpleasant things that could happen when you go.

For a lot of kids, the absolute worst thing that happens involves needles. Vaccinations are incredibly important for staying healthy, but that doesn't make the needle stick any more fun. In fact,

We tend to focus on the negative, but a lot of good things happen at hospitals, too.

EDUCATIONAL VIDEO

Scan this code for a video about hospitals' efforts to help kids stop fearing hospitals.

Opposite: The fear of needles is one of the most common of all.

needle phobia (or "trypanophobia") is a pretty big problem—as many as 1 in 10 adults has it. And of that group, about one fifth avoid medical treatment simply because of the needles.

Other people are uncomfortable with the fact that they have to undress and be touched

PHOBIAS

A phobia is a very intense fear of a very specific thing. If someone has a phobia, he or she gets extremely upset when exposed to the scary thing—far more upset than the situation seems to require. In addition, the fear interferes with their life in some way. For instance, someone might refuse to go to school because of a fear of fire drills. There are lots of different medical phobias and they often have more than one name. Here are some of them:

- agliophobia: fear of pain.
- bacteriophobia, germophobia, mysophobia: fear of germs.
- carcinophobia: fear of cancer.
- emetophobia: fear of throwing up.
- hemophobia, hematophobia: fear of blood.
- iatrophobia: fear of doctors.
- nosocomephobia: fear of hospitals.
- thanatophobia: fear of death.
- trypanophobia: fear of needles.

Keep in mind that having some amount fear of a particular thing does not mean you have a phobia. For example, most people fear death, but that doesn't mean they all have thanatophobia. The fear has to interfere with your daily life in some way.

by someone they don't know well. This may feel embarrassing, but it's important to remember that doctors and nurses are just trying to make sure that you are okay. They touch lots of strangers as part of their work, and they aren't going to judge you or laugh at you.

Some people don't mind the touching or even the needles, but medical tests make them anxious. A doctor or nurse might take a blood or urine sample, or even a skin sample sometimes, and have it analyzed to find out if there is any medical problem. This is really upsetting to some people, but for

Medical tests sometimes involve strange equipment that can make people nervous.

different reasons. Some of the tests that adults need to take are not much fun. The colonoscopy, which examines the internal organs involved in digesting and eliminating food, is the most famous example. Other people are afraid of medical tests because they tend to assume the worst. They assume they have whatever illness the test is looking for. Sometimes they get upset about a diagnosis they haven't even gotten yet.

Fortunately, for most people, these fears are minor. But as we mentioned in chapter one, these types of medical fears can keep people from getting the treatment they need. For example, if a colonoscopy finds cancer at an early stage, the survival rate is over 90 percent. But if someone avoids the test, the cancer may not be found. Doctors can't fix problems that they don't know about.

RESEARCH PROJECT

Choose one of the phobias listed in the sidebar and find out more about it. Write a story based on your research about a person who has that phobia. What does the person do to avoid the fear? How does it affect his or her life?

TEXT-DEPENDENT QUESTIONS

1. Why do some people fear hospitals?

2. What scares some people about the doctor's office?

3. What's a name for the fear of needles?

CHAPTER FOUR

CONQUERING MEDICAL FEARS

Few things are more frustrating than when you are upset about something, and another person says, "Oh, just get over it." When it comes to anxiety, we know it's not that simple.

However, that doesn't mean you're helpless. There are a number of things you can do to take charge and stop being so afraid of medical issues. It may not be easy, but it is doable.

TALK AND LEARN

Step one: talk about it. Silence is not your friend in this situation. Pretending the problem does not exist will not help you fix it. You certainly don't have to tell everybody you know! But you do need to find at least one person you can trust and talk to.

It can be nerve-wracking to admit to being afraid, especially if you think your fears are silly. But remember, your fears are not silly. The best way to begin the process of defeating them is to admit

WORDS TO UNDERSTAND

infectious: a disease that can be passed from one person to another.

sanitation: a set of conditions, including a sewage system and clean water, that improves health.

sedative: medicine that makes people relax or fall asleep.

triggered: caused a strong reaction.

that they exist. Then you can make a plan about what to do.

If you feel comfortable, a parent or guardian is a good place to start. But the key person to tell is your doctor. Don't assume your doctor doesn't care or will think your fears are dumb. After all, it's doctor's job to help you be as healthy as possible. So if you are suffering from anxiety about medicine, your doctor is the perfect person to assist you! And if this book has shown you anything, it's that you are not alone. It's impossible that you are the first person with medical fears that your doctor has ever encountered. In fact, it happens all the time.

Even if it's embarrassing, tell your doctor or nurse about your fears. They want to help!

MEDICAL FEAR OR ANXIETY DISORDER?

When you discuss your medical fears, your doctor may want to also talk about anxiety in your life generally. It's possible that your medical fears are actually part of a larger challenge with anxiety. (See books in this set called *Phobias* and *Symptoms and Treatments of Anxiety Disorders* for more information.)

Doctors are very good at helping people in general, so they are going to want to help you with being afraid, too.

Second, educate yourself. Reading this book means you are off to a good start! Your doctor can probably recommend good sources of information about anxiety—both as a general idea and specifically as it relates to medicine. There are also more suggestions at the back of this book.

MAKE SPECIFIC PLANS

Another reason why you should talk to your doctor is that he or she can take concrete steps to make your visits easier. For example, the office might be able to adjust your appointments in such a way that the waiting room is less busy, or the line is shorter. If it's the exam room or dentist's chair that bothers you, perhaps it would help to spend a little time there when you don't have an appointment, so that you can get used to it. An anxiety specialist named Dr.

EDUCATIONAL VIDEO

Scan this code for a video with tips about conquering fear.

Opposite: Bring something along to distract you while you wait for the appointment.

David Carbonell tells a story about a woman whose fears were triggered by the white coat her dentist wore. After she finally told him about it, the dentist agreed to ditch the coat and wear his regular clothes when she comes in for her appointment.

A major reason people have medical fears is because we fear the unknown. We might fear a medical procedure because we don't know what will happen, how long it will last, or how much it will hurt. You'd be surprised how often people have procedures or tests without really understanding what is being done. Usually this is because they don't want to ask too many questions. Go ahead and ask the questions! Having some answers will probably make you feel better.

You could also try deep-breathing exercises or learning how to meditate in order to help calm your nerves while in the waiting room. Another trick is to make sure you bring a lot of distractions with you. You could listen to music with headphones, play on an electronic device like a phone or tablet, or read a good book. Bring several different options to the appointment to keep your mind busy while you wait.

Some dentists give patients a sedative to help them relax in the chair. That is not always done for kids, but it is used sometimes, so you might ask your doctor if that is an option for you.

Another thing that helps some people is to promise themselves a reward later. They think,

"Okay, if I make it through this dentist appointment, then afterwards I can go do X." (The X stands for whatever the person's favorite thing is.) Having a reward waiting gives the brain something positive to focus on.

There is another benefit to rewards: they help you remember that there *is* going to be a period called "after this doctor's appointment." Your

THERAPIST APPOINTMENT

Going to see a therapist for the first time can be scary. Again, it's a case of fearing the unknown. So here is a little primer on therapists:

- **Who are they?** There are many types of therapists. Some are called psychologists and some are psychiatrists. The main difference between the two is the amount of medical training they have, and whether or not they can prescribe drugs to their patients—which psychiatrists can do, but psychologists cannot. There are also social workers, counselors, and psychotherapists—they all have slightly different types of training and areas of expertise.

- **What do they do?** All mental health professionals are trained to help people with issues relating to their minds: their thoughts, their fears, their emotions, and their relationships with others.

- **How do they do it?** There are many different types of therapy. The most famous, sometimes called "talk therapy," simply involves sitting in a room and discussing your feelings. The therapist will guide the discussion in ways that help the patient learn about themselves and others. There are also more active types of therapy where patients practice particular skills to help them cope with their problems.

appointment is really just one small moment in a long life.

Sometimes it helps to remind yourself that the doctor has many other patients to see that day. And the dentist is going to look at a lot of other people's teeth besides yours. Focus on the fact that it will end. A woman named Virginia Lounsbury developed a severe doctor phobia after having a

- **Where do they do it?** That depends on the type of therapist. Some have their own private offices, while others work at hospitals, schools, or other institutions.
- **What's it like?** Again, the answer to this depends on the type of therapy. You might see your therapist once a week, or possibly more, depending on the situation. There are no tests or procedures like there are with other types of doctors—you do not have to undress, for example. However, you might have homework! Sometimes therapists have patients work on particular skills, such as relaxation techniques, and those skills need to be practiced before the next appointment.

In group therapy, people share their struggles and offer support to one another.

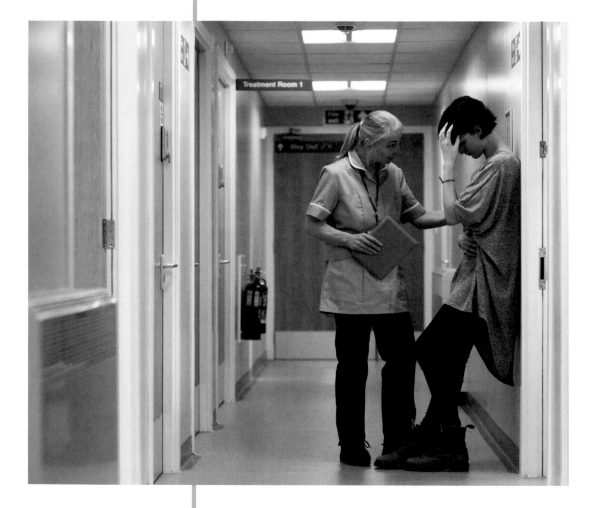

It can be scary when someone you love is in the hospital.

lot of health problems. But she reminds herself that "it's only temporary. Nobody has ever gone to the doctor forever."

THE GOOD NEWS

We are better informed about health than ever before. But that knowledge has a dark side. Bad things have always happened, but now we know about more of them. Sometimes it can be helpful to take a step back and look at history.

In 1900, the average life expectancy of Americans was less than 50 years. The major causes of death were infectious diseases. The major cause of death among young women was childbirth. There were no antibiotics, and a number of "cures" for various illnesses were actually toxic.

Today, the average life expectancy of Americans is nearly 80 years. Vaccinations keep some of our worst illnesses at bay, sanitation keeps infections from spreading, and plentiful food helps us stay healthier overall. None of the top killers from 1900 are major problems in the Western world. Yes, people still get sick, and people still die. Doctors are human: they make mistakes sometimes, and they can't fix every problem. For all our knowledge about illness, there is still much that we need to learn.

Medical fears are not going away, because there is nothing more human that fearing illness and death. But in all of human history, there has never been a safer time to go to the doctor, have dental work, or visit a hospital.

RESEARCH PROJECT

Create a pamphlet that a pediatrician might keep in his or her office with advice for kids who have medical fears. Use the information in this book, in the Further Reading section, and other material you find yourself. If possible, ask the school nurse or your own doctor for suggestions. If the pamphlet turns out well, offer it to your doctor or school nurse for them to use!

TEXT-DEPENDENT QUESTIONS

1. What's the most important thing people with medical fears should do?

2. What are some tips that might make appointments less scary?

3. What should someone expect from his or her first visit to a therapist?

FURTHER READING

Colgate Oral Care Center. "What Is Dental Anxiety and Phobia?" http://www.colgate.com/en/us/oc/oral-health/basics/dental-visits/ article/what-is-dental-anxiety-and-phobia.

Esposito, Lisa. "How to Overcome Extreme Fear of Doctors." *U.S. News & World Report*, July 1, 2014. http://health.usnews.com/health-news/ patient-advice/articles/2014/07/01/how-to-overcome-extreme-fear-of-doctors.

KidsHealth. "Going to a Psychologist, Psychiatrist, or Therapist." https://kidshealth.org/en/kids/going-to-therapist.html.

Port, Dina Roth. "7 Tips to Help Kids Overcome Fear of Doctors." *Parents*. http://www.parents.com/health/doctors/kids-overcome-fear-doctors/.

Sine, Richard. "Beyond 'White Coat Syndrome.'" WebMD. http://www.webmd.com/anxiety-panic/features/ beyond-white-coat-syndrome.

EDUCATIONAL VIDEOS

Chapter One: Psych Videos. "What to Do about Medical Phobias." https://youtu.be/ZB6TOdeaOal.

Chapter Two: WISE Channel. "Simulation Surgery Helps Portuguese Kids Conquer Fear of Doctors." https://youtu.be/Hr0CVL6e7jM.

Chapter Three: The Better Show. "Easing Hospital Fears." https://youtu.be/U8d5AgcCFk4.

Chapter Four: Watchwellcast. "5 Tricks for Overcoming Fear." https://youtu.be/GDjwfFmXwfE.

SERIES GLOSSARY

adaptive: a helpful response to a particular situation.

bias: a feeling against a particular thing or idea.

biofeedback: monitoring of bodily functions with the goal of learning to control those functions.

cognitive: relating to the brain and thought.

comorbid: when one illness or disorder is present alongside another one.

context: the larger situation in which an event takes place.

diagnose: to identify an illness or disorder.

exposure: having contact with something.

extrovert: a person who enjoys being with others.

harassment: picking on another person frequently and deliberately.

hypnosis: creating a state of consciousness where someone is awake but highly open to suggestion.

inhibitions: feelings that restricts what we do or say.

introvert: a person who prefers being alone.

irrational: baseless; something that's not connected to reality.

melatonin: a substance that helps the body regulate sleep.

milestone: an event that marks a stage in development.

motivating: something that makes you want to work harder.

occasional: from time to time; not often.

panic attack: sudden episode of intense, overwhelming fear.

paralyzing: something that makes you unable to move (can refer to physical movement as well as emotions).

peers: people who are roughly the same age as you.

perception: what we see and believe to be true.

persistent: continuing for a noticeable period.

phobia: extreme fear of a particular thing.

preventive: keeping something from happening.

probability: the likelihood that a particular thing will happen.

psychological: having to do with the mind and thoughts.

rational: based on a calm understanding of facts, rather than emotion.

sedative: a type of drug that slows down bodily processes, making people feel relaxed or even sleepy.

self-conscious: overly aware of yourself, to the point that it makes you awkward.

serotonin: a chemical in the brain that is important in moods.

stereotype: an oversimplified idea about a type of person that may not be true for any given individual.

stigma: a sense of shame or disgrace associated with a particular state of being.

stimulant: a group of substances that speed up bodily processes.

subconscious: thoughts and feelings you have but may not be aware of.

syndrome: a condition.

treatable: describes a medical condition that can be healed.

upheaval: a period of great change or uncertainty.

INDEX

agoraphobia 9–10

anxiety 17, 21, 22, 35, 36

anxiety disorder 37

appointments

    advice about 20, 41

    avoiding 13

avoidance 14, 22, 33

colonoscopy 27, 33

confidentiality 20

dentists 16, 20, 41

    fear of, 11, 13, 19, 22–23, 38

    honesty and 20

doctors

    fear of 11–12, 19–22

    honesty 20, 21

exams, fear of 12–13, 32–34

hospitals, fear of 12, 13–14, 27–29, 30, 42

illness, fear of 10–11

judgment, fear of 20–21, 32

life expectancy 43

medical fears

    advice about 16–17, 35–42

    symptoms of 13

needles, fear of 14, 16, 27, 29–31

office, medical, fear of 12, 13, 16, 23, 37

phobias 30, 41

preventive care 9, 14, 15

relaxation 38

rewards 38–40

therapists 40–41

therapists

    advice about 20

    fear of 24–25

    types of 40

touching, fear of 13, 30–32

trypanophobia 30

undressing, fear of 12–13, 30–32

unknown, fear of 38

vaccinations 14, 15, 29, 43

white-coat syndrome 19

ABOUT THE ADVISOR

Anne S. Walters is Clinical Associate Professor of Psychiatry and Human Behavior at the Alpert Medical School of Brown University. She is also Chief Psychologist for Bradley Hospital. She is actively involved in teaching activities within the Clinical Psychology Training Programs of the Alpert Medical School and serves as Child Track Seminar Co-Coordinator. Dr. Walters completed her undergraduate work at Duke University, graduate school at Georgia State University, internship at UTexas Health Science Center, and postdoctoral fellowship at Brown University.

ABOUT THE AUTHOR

H. W. Poole is a writer and editor of books for young people, including the sets, *Families Today* and *Mental Illnesses and Disorders: Awareness and Understanding* (Mason Crest). She created the *Horrors of History* series (Charlesbridge) and the *Ecosystems* series (Facts On File). She has also been responsible for many critically acclaimed reference books, including *Political Handbook of the World* (CQ Press) and the *Encyclopedia of Terrorism* (SAGE). She was coauthor and editor of *The History of the Internet* (ABC-CLIO), which won the 2000 American Library Association RUSA award.

PHOTO CREDITS